1

Semper fi

By Ivan D. Villaluz and
Rosario B. Villaluz

Edited by Ayo Gutierrez
Illustrated by Ssareeta Singh

Philippine Copyright
by GMGA Publishing
May 2020
ISBN: 9798645243777

About the Book

Semper Fi,

"Always Faithful"

is a collection of
verses and poems
about
faith
hope
love
and how these three
matter
in the journey of life.

Reviews

Semper Fi, is a book written by the poets of today, Ivan and Rosario Villaluz.

If you're looking for a book that speaks the feelings hidden in the little chambers of your heart, this is your must-read.

You wonder, what makes a poet write lines that speak to you? What compels a poet to collect their thoughts and write a book about their faith, their fears, their love, and their aspirations?

The first few pages will make you realize how much we all need the Almighty in our lives. The freeverse tone makes the works easy to internalize and you reflect upon your own. The play of words used in every line tugs at the heart.

Enjoy every word as you progress at every poetry. "Endless Love" will make you fall in love with your significant other, all over again. "My Voice They Know" speaks of your tender feelings towards your children.

In a simple answer, they wrote the book "to preserve their legacy." Ideal reason!

The great thing about this book is that towards the end is the poem "All Will Be Well", poetry that brings glory to God, despite all the hardships and challenges this life has made us experience.

The Villaluz descendants would surely be grateful for this work of art. I couldn't be more thankful enough to have read the book myself. It will give you a deep understanding of life in poetry. It allows you to stop, and reflect, bringing about your consciousness, as if you are the one who mediated on each of the lines.

It's simple. It's perfect. A book for keeps!

Edellen Reyes
Direct Response Copywriter

Enlightening and uplifting… from the weight of holiness to hope and love. Their words offer us a different kind of light that will surely pull you out from the dark. The poems are very honest and never lose wonder in delivering its message. It is best to read aloud to those people whom we wanted to welcome in delight. It makes a good addition when you want to gain spiritually and to love again.

Jacquelou Magante aka Aki
Author of *unsent; archived*

"… in as much as they are faithful, lo, I will be with them even unto the end. "- D & C 75:13

Awakening, spiritual, thought- nourishing and converting! Semper fi, a Latin phrase which means 'always faithful ', a book by Ivan and Rosario Villaluz, is considered as the maxim of poetry. Faith is the critical virtue most required if anyone wants to fathom this book. It takes to have faith in order to decipher the spiritual verses of the authors. The Villaluzes were able to mention God many times in their poems. Their verses are like spiritual thoughts that nourish the soul.

Their poems convey that we must always be faithful in our continuous tides of life to reach the distant shore. We must always have faith to test us in times of affliction, and that we must have the amor to our fellowmen because love is the greatest thing, loving others is the same as loving God. Reading this book will inspire us to strengthen and magnify our faith.

--Danny Gallardo Co-author of Bards from the Far East: Anthology of Haiku and Kindred Verses

Semper Fi which translates to *Always Faithful* is truly an apt title for this anthology where the poetries are mostly composed with the faith in God and love, and it has never been evasive in its journey.

The words chosen are simple but profound; they convey the right dose of emotion which has made this anthology so likeable. The concise but crisp nature of composition has enhanced the reading value since it has shown successfully what the poets intended to show rather than trying to tell something elaborately.

I truly wish all the very best to Ivan and Rosario for many more endeavors towards composing their exceptionally honest and romantic poetries.

-Som Mazunder, an avid Reader

Foreword

The beginning is an initiative of one's mind to correct moment to begin. The mindset of the Poets— to be in an adventure to world of words with flourishing ideas upon imaginative spell into poetry— is like a song in rhythm with heart: to belong.

A compelling thinking to do what the heart is paying rapt attention to, so too with poems: The chemistry must rhyme with the minds of the Poets; the verbatims must dazzle into souls to be admired, of which all the verses created have relatable meaning; there should be noticeable approach to publish those composed poems in a book, with sweet formula employed, making every single poem with breathtaking quality, right from the opening line; and the verses should be always in silent spiritual under- current pulsation underneath every line, rewarding the readers intangible enrichment, apart from satisfying senses. Credibility be grasped by readers with those sensibilities of virtues presented.

And, that formula is transcribed, glibly in this book Semper Fi (Always Faithful). With the faithfulness from the authors'– Ivan and Rosario Villaluz – hearts and minds conspired to Ars Poetica. Their perspective from their minds, that gray matters perceptions matter into phrases to be praised. Thusly this book of collaboration is noteworthy to ponder.

Ency Bearis, RN, Poet, Author

Acknowledgment

To our direct ascendants
Papa Adolfo and Mama Vianney
Papa Samson and Mama Trinidad
and Ninay Caridad

To our siblings
Antonia, Marcela, Emmanuel and Christie

To our angels in disguise
Gabrielle, Raphaelle and Matthew

To the Fairy Bard, Ayo Gutierrez
And to the rest of the amazing bards from the Far
East

Colleagues
Friends
and
Kins.

You continue to give us reasons
to believe in faith, hope, and love especially in times
of afflictions.

Above all to our Creator
for His unfailing manifestation of Divine orchestration
To God be all the glory and praise.

Table of Contents

12

Semper Fi, In initio

At the prime of their youth
Their paths once crossed
It was just short-lived
They pursue different routes

Beyond the future unknown
He struggled with his faith
Oftentimes on the brink
Yet preserved it, he remains

She's got fair share of tastes of fate
And a series of tests of faith,
At times beyond her strength
Without fear even from death

Both wrestle with their co-existence
While taking roads winding and diverse
He was praying for one true love to come
She was praying for only one man to love

And when the stars in the heavens collide
Both got most of the stardusts in their hair
Somewhere down the road less trodden
Their paths crossed all over again

What are the chances they will meet?
It is almost nil, they concede
But can't discount what destiny creates
When Someone Divine orchestrates

Everything falls into its place
Amazing fates and coincidences!
With ovewhelming love and faith
They sealed a lifetime promise

To love and to behold
In their youth till old
To love and to cherish
In prosperity and austerity

When the storm is at its tempest
Embracing the worst and the best
Oblivious of what tomorrow brings
As long as they hold their hands

And as these two souls valiantly face
With exuding love, hope and faith
The beaming rays of the rising sun
The waning sunlit of the setting sun

Nothing will never go wrong
While holding each other's hand
Keeping the faith from above
And rejoicing unrivaled love

Fate has its share of twists and sweet coincidences
These two souls revel in weaving poetry at its best
Poems after poems carefully gathered over the years
Gave birth to one perfect collaboration

Finally wrap it up into this book of poems and verses.
Semper Fi
a collection of poetry
about faith, hope and love
and how these three matter especially in times of
afflictions
came into being.

Life's a Poem

Poetry is life
Beyond the voice of angels
It's the heart of God

In nature man finds
Tranquility and solace
Rebirth for the soul

Birds' songs in the air
Still the troubled heart of man
Enkindles the fire

Flowers in the fields
Bring out rainbows of life
Hues of glorious hope

Whispering wind blows
Gently tickling li'l leaves
Asking man to dance

Racing drops of rain
Wanting to touch the meadow
Reflect man's great quest

Life's indeed a poem
Where God's the greatest writer
Hid in a poet

Fides

Fides Cordis

Heart does not have eyes to see
But it believes in you and me.
It braves to tread the road
Even though it seems so broad.
It simply draws out fides within
In life's journey through thick and thin.
Fides sets its arrows beyond the horizon
Keeping the heart beating on.
When strength fades away a bit
It gives the eyes its glow and gilt.
Fides cordis
Believes in Divine's bliss
It is as sweet as honey on
Love's first kiss.
When you have faith in your heart
Never abandon nor let Her depart.

Day by Day

Dear God,

Day by day,
    Your ways amaze me
Day by day,
    Your peace appeases me
Day by day,
    Your help amuses me
Day by day,
    Your love sustains me
Because day by day,
    You showed me how much

                    You love me.

No Matter What

One night I had a dream
Having a rare encounter with the Lord
The scene was very dim,
I was groping for something I could hold.

At last, there came out a ray of light
I opened my eyes to a room overly bright
Then a ladder appeared in sight
Yet I had no idea what's the purpose for that.

Suddenly, I heard a soft voice
"My child, all you have to do is climb."
And I just followed even when I was confused
All my uncertainties I left behind.

When I was halfway the flight, the ladder trembled
I began to worry I might fall
I started to seek safety on my own
And forgot the God I've known.

"My child, hold on, just hold on.
Everything will be fine soon."
I was overcome with a flood of relief
I didn't have to worry about myself.

Life is just like that:
The storms come, and we feel their wrath
Day and night, our tears testify
We hang on a tightrope, for our lives we fight.

Remember God is always there
Good things come to those He holds dear
All we must do is believe and trust Him
No matter how strong the storm may seem

Make Me a Servant

I have the feeling today
And to this reality I stay:

Reminding myself to be selfless
In the exigency of the service
For the glory of God and to others

And may the prayer of my heart will always be:
Make me a servant to Thee

Mornight Monologue

Half the world's sleeping
Half the world's awake
Cicadas sound's deafening
Dogs occasionally growling

Hubby and kiddos snoring
And here I am again, and again
Half awake and half asleep
My coffee's brewing

In this cold evening
Keyboards and mouse clicking
Files, references, piling
Mind's wandering, bewildering

O'er research, auditing, marketing
Nonetheless with great thanksgiving
To the great Almighty
For getting me by and by

When Glory's Gone

A man prayed that he'd reach the top.
God said, "Sure, I would put you up."
Then, he prayed that he'd be the best.
And God said, "Sure, you'd be the best."

He prayed that he would win the race.
God said, "Sure, you will win the race."
The man prayed that he'd have the crown.
And God said, "Sure, a golden crown."

The man prayed that he'd soar the skies.
God said, "Sure, like a bird that flies."
Then, he prayed that he'd never sigh.
God said, "Sure, you will never cry."

Then, the man looked down from above.
"What can you see down from above?"
"People as tiny as the sand."
"Do you think they'd see you from land?"

"Yes, I suppose they could see me."
"You think you're big for them to see."
"Thank you, Lord, for putting me here."
What gain have you now that you're here?"

The man paused and thought for a while.
"Engrossed with pride your heart sees li'l.
Thinking that you're bigger than them.
You forget that they're your brothers."

Don't you know that for them you're small?
Watch your heart or else you will fall.
Learn from great men who lived the earth.
Humility was their sole wealth.

Abase yourself and you'll be wise.
Be glad when you see others rise.
For you have said my will be done,
Be grateful still when glory's gone."

October'ries

October is the Month of Rosary
But this October comes in a special way
Because I love. I Live.
Life is indeed full of mysteries
And here is the litany
I got a crucial role in the life of a lost friend
So down that a dear friend's marriage gets rocky
Glad to meet this "Claytown's poor lady"
Who became the official spiritual confidante
And got funny bones too to bring us smileys
Got courageous to sign up to "Freedom from Debt
Coalition"
Was amazed to realize that I have that
entrepreneurial bones
"Certified" promoting Pro-Life Advocacy
Got stucked between two giants fighting with might
And today, same month, four years ago
God entrusted to me one of His angels on earth
My everdearest Raphaelle,
Co-celebrating the feast of dear St. Raphael
Whose birthday wish is just a piece of cake
With icings and her name on it
Is this wish more than enough to make me going?
Life is indeed beautiful and funny
If it has its Sorrowful Mysteries
Joyful, Light, and Glorious Mysteries
Are also surely coming its way

The faith of a child

Many are the seeds in this world
But there's this seed that's hard to grow.
Some tried to plant yet many failed
Though they're wise and thought they knew.

Early should man start if he wants.
Growing this seed starts early morn.
Midday scorches the seed man plants.
Midnight's late for strength's lost and worn.

Water this daily with Patience.
Prune it till you see the twigs
And be amazed of its radiance
With its fruits better than figs.

Only little children know this seed
Trust like them with faith when in need.

Charis

Light had I none
Nor life was with me.
Emptiness was all I had
And uncertainty was my guide.

A gift I never asked
Nor expected grace to have.
His great love brought me light
And life to me He gave.

Never had I known His name
Nor had I known His ways
But the Advocate to me He sent
And granted me faith to believe.

Reason have I now to hope
For life eternal He holds.
Peace I know He will grant
For this soul which He loves.

Amare

Amorem Ex Animo

Hear this beautiful song
To sing this to you I long.
Its rhythmic beat and angelic melody
Blended in the sweetest harmony.

Let the flowers in the field
To thy beauty yield.
Let the stars in the night
Give their radiant light.

Amore ex animo
Let it be shared by me and you.
Even if a nightingale forgets its song
Still in my heart you belong.

I bless the Heavens above
For giving such a great love.

My Voice They Know

My dearest children, to me your Mother listen
I now am weary and heavily laden
The past they forget and the present they ruin
Strength now fails me, and I am now in dire pain
Withhold not your balm to me --your Mother-- that I may
live again

Stand and be strong in times of ordeal
Keep your light aglow and don't let anybody steal
For thy Mother's sake blow your horns and let your
brothers feel
That without Me they all will bear the ill
For time will come that I will be for them hard as steel

The youthful blood that runs on your vein
I have kept and preserved for time from vain
My dearly loved children, to me your Mother remain
The virtues instilled in your hearts preserve from stain
Or else you will be like them who are insane.

Draw your strength from God and reveal
Your precious talent and use your skill
Shout no war cries on the hill
But rather shout for joy, and then chaos will be brought to a
standstill
Be the key in changing the course of the journey by being
the master of the wheel.

May God give you the strength of Samson
That you may build the pillars again like a true mason
May wisdom, too, be yours like Solomon
To take the lead and face the vast new horizon
Don't be like them who run in frantic like lunatics during
full moon

Refuse the Poison they are trying to let you drink
My dearest children, I pray, you think
And ever be as lovely roses, pink
I love you and to me you are more precious than silver
chink
I have ever watched you and I have not made even a single
wink

I reminded them of the past to contemplate on
Yet they learn not and loved their state forlorn
How I wished they were not to me born
Because to me they turn to assault and treason
Their hearts are swollen with pride and are adamant to
govern

Remember thy heroes' blood which was used as ink
To mark the pact and for you to drink
Freedom they have fought which caused the stars to blink
They never allowed their hope and loyalty down the sea
sink
Let yourselves be like conductors of love and energy like
zinc

My only hope I found alone in you
For past had passed and never will become new
Make the most of your gift for the hour is long due
That you, the Promised Youth will come into view
Whatever you do, wherever you go, keep your teachable
hearts anew

My children, thy banner let it stand and wave.
Set it high with pride for you are no longer the slave.
Come out from the dungeon and the dark cave.
Muster and curb your spirit and never rave
Stand with conviction and be brave

I plea my children be the dew
To their lips and tongue taste like stew
In your eyes reflect Red, White and Blue,
A reflection of a long past hue
My dearest youth, waver not and stand like evergreen yew

Remember the blessed names of heroes on the grave
Follow their footsteps and like them behave
Abhor the ravenous contemporary leaders that crave
For power, glory and riches to Hell they save
Healing, peace, love and justice, these you should pave

Fight for justice and fight for your right
But never retreat rather till death you fight
My last hope I found in your might
Young you may be yet endowed by God with wisdom and
light
My dearest youth, amidst the dark keep your candles alight

Keep your hands busy and blameless
Of prejudices, injustices, selfishness and grudges
Keep your hearts clean and shameless
Of envy, hatred, pride and covetousness
My dear children keep your minds holy, pure and free from
iniquities

Think of the past like the moonless midnight
This will be your future if today your only weapon is flight
My beloved children never lose your sight
From the virtues which God takes delight
Then all will be Day and there will be no more Night

Uphold my precious Name and show your prowess
Build the future today with the spirit of willingness
For in your hands lie the future boundless
Love me and heal me with your love so pure and endless
For through me God will pour his blessings, banish all your
bitterness and grant you peace.

Love

Triumphant over yesterday's ordeal
Unusual incomparable woman
Illumined like light giving ideal,
Vigor, epigrammatic mortal yarn.

Love overruled, virulent emptiness.
Misty years recede; obscurity stilled.
Absolute repose incited us best
Dance Eros' artistry revivified.

I forever owe unwonted naïve
Dedication, great respect equable.
Adhere to love's orders, virtues. Evolve
In natty yoke of unpredictable

Uranus. Now, time isn't lachrymose
For our reveries end Valentine's Rose

Time of My Day

At five o'clock
my alarm clock starts
I try to go back
Anyway, it's still dark

At five-fifteen
It's the alarm again
I attempt to sleep quietly
Must be up or be tardy

At five-thirty, things got to be ready
I say my prayers shortly
Compelled to be a good cook
By hook or by crook

Now the clock spins six
Sponge down the dishes
Get rid of all the mess
Ensure no stain is missed

At six-thirty
I pack lunch for kids and daddy
While nibbling bread
And sipping a cup of coffee

Now it's quarter to seven
Got to dip the kiddies
Though their eyes still half open
They must get up to be school-ready

At seven-thirty
Off to work I must hurry
A sign of a breather
As I say another prayer

At exactly eight
I fulfill my duties for the state
Between eight to five
Being a good servant, I strive

Directions from bosses
Clients giving buzzes
Follow up here
Follow up there

Some days are light and gaily
Without so much to worry
Some days are filled with fuzz
Yet no haze so immense will last

At the end of the day
Earning the day's pay
And making a difference
Is an enormous recompense

At six, heading home already
Another round of household duty
Homework and pillow fights
Kiddies playing with their might

At past seven
Sharing tales to my kids is my haven
Hearing them laugh is the best
My antidote to worry and stress

Before I lay down my head to rest
I find innermost bliss and peace
Taking account of how I spend my time
To the one who is worthy and divine

This Heart of Mine

In times of uncertainties I never have asked nor
complained
Vulnerable I may be, yet, I never ceased to grope and
move,
Amidst great mountains and endless horizon,
Never have I questioned heaven for such an ordeal.

Years I wearily tread the winding road, yet I kept a
cheerful heart

Rest evaded me until this heart finds its haven
Overwhelmed with such a pure love sent from above,
Salve has been poured upon and healed the wound
Aurora has lit these eyes after the darkest times.
Rivulet has soothed this parched and weakened
heart.

Imagine how great the Source of Love is
Overflowing joy has dawned and was granted to this
heart of mine.

Sigh No More

Sigh no more dear heart, and be merry
I have given you my soul, my lady
Distance may be too far for our love to cross
But I am with you through prayers
Kisses and hugs I may have been suppressed
But my affection will never cease
Be at peace my love for I know heaven's grace isn't withheld
But rather delayed--
Testing our love's endurance and our faith
Heaven hears our plea and will make us free

Speak to Me, My Love

Speak to me my love
Speak to me my love
Say the words I long to hear
Your silence deafens my heart

Break thy lips that could quench my longing
Your absence weakens my arms, for they are made
to hold you tight
I long for your sweet glances that could ease my
burning passion
My lady, answer me and let your answer resound in
the corners of my heart

To you I give my purest love
For you I spend my life, my love

Wife

When and If Failures Exist ... You are there to understand.
When and If Felicity is Estranged ... You are there to make things light.
When and If Family is Endangered... You are there as a strong shield.
When and If Fortitude is Evading... You are there as a pillar of stone.
When and If Feebleness is Enraged ... You are there to bring tranquility.
When and If Fickleness is Engaged... You are there as the light.
When and If Forgiveness is Empty... You are there to endure.
When and If Flame is Encountered... You run deep and cool.
When and If Flowers are Expiring... You are there to give hope.
When and If Friendship is Elusive... You are there with your heart.
When and If Fatherhood is Erring... You are there to empathize.
When and If Frigidity is Enormous... You are there like the sun.

I'd Rather Be

I'd rather be mute
If my tongue refuses to say I love you
I'd rather be without arms
if I don't have yours interlocked with mine
I'd rather be without feet
if you refuse to take a walk with me
I'd rather be dumb
if you stop whispering the words I long to hear
I'd rather be dead
if you turn and walk away
I'd rather be blind
than have eyes that can't gaze upon you
I'd rather be a fool in love
than sensible without affection
I'd rather die
than live without your love

Nothingness is all I have
without you in my life

Till You Came

I was never like me till you came
I was like a rainbow so pale in the vast skies
I was like the moon behind the clouds
I was like the sun that refuses its rays to illumine
I was like the wind so aimless in the fields
I was like the river, turbulent and too shallow
I was like a door without a knob
I was like a mute shouting in the streets
I was like a ship without a rudder
I was like a bird without wings
I was like a garden so empty
I was never like me till you came to stay with me

Grace to forever treasure
From the God who's the greatest of all.

Endless Love

I've got a feeling it's you I wanted
I don't know deep inside if you felt the same way too
I've long waited to show my feelings for you
But I was afraid our friendship wouldn't survive this
flow.

Yet God works in ways we cannot see
Where our efforts falter, He surely finds a way
For when He led you to me
I knew that I found my destiny.

It's you I've been thinking every night and day
You're always in my mind even if I'm far away
How I wished we could be together someday
And realized our dream of building a family.

I knew I loved you even from the start
And I prayed we would never part
I will love you for the rest of my life
Endless love is all I can promise, my love.

Summer Diaries

Day 1   At the break of dawn
         On this early morn
         Thanking the One and Almighty
         For today's another day!

Day 2   Mr. Sun, Mr. Sun!
         You seem to be hiding out there!
         Please show up, Mr. Sun!
         Little Ella and Liane!
         Don't want to miss the fun!

Day 3   Oh, look at the sun!
         It's shining up there!
         Oh, Mother, Mother!
         Little Ella and Liane!
         Just wanna have some fun!

Day 4   Sailing
         Sailing
         Summer fun
         Summer fun
         Under the sun
         Under the sun

Day 5   Seashells, seashells!
         Such cute sea creatures!
         Such a gift of nature!
         No matter how big or small!

Day 6   Nature's wave breakers
Fringing reefs, that is
These are coral reefs along the shore
Similar to barrier reefs and atolls

Day 7   Where the dark blue southern seas
Kiss the dark sand and corals
Where the water and earth
Gladly meet

Day 8   Welcome aboard Captain Shan Carby
Fasten your seat belt passenger,
Raphaelle Marie
Off to the deep blue southern seas
Off to the other side of the world to see

Day 9   Kids always imitate
Kids always innovate
Kids always find happiness
Mostly in simplest things!

Day 10   Hello, cute little piglet!
Also want to have some fun!
Basking under the smiling sun!
Such a cute little pet
Her bathroom is the vast beach
Since birth!

Bohol

Sa akong pagkahidagsa sa Bohol Island
Daghan kaajo kong angay pasalamatan
Naka eye to eye ko sa talagsaon nga tarsier
Nakatungas ako sa Chocolate Hills
Abi ko makaon dili man diay
Apan may lamian dinhi nga ube ug kalamay
Relaxing kaajo ang Loboc river cruise
Inubanan sa mabugnaw nga buko juice
Naa dinhi ang kinakaraanang simbahan sa Baclayon
Usab puti kaajo ang balas sa mga baybayon
Apan ang dako ko uyamot nga pasalamat
Ang buotan nga Bol anon ako nahimamat
Mao nga dako nakong pasalamat sa Kahitas-an
Iya kong gipadpad dinhi sa Bohol Island

Inner Peace, Inner Peace

No party balloons and poppers
Only masks and nebulizers
No marshmallows and cakes
Only fruits and veggies

No venues or halls for parties
Only quiet rooms and hallways
No children's shouts and laughter
Only this child's wisdom and vigor

No crying, no complaining
Only inner joy and thanksgiving
To the Almighty King
Ever caring, ever loving

Just Around the Bend

No mountain is so high which can hinder you from my
sight
No ocean so deep can fathom my love's depth
No sky so vast can surmount affection
We may be separated by seas and mountains
But if we keep this love and faith alive
We will be more than sustained

And the moment when we could be together
May just be around the bend

Sibling Revelries

Gabrielle is meticulously prim and proper.
Raphaelle is sporty, sometimes doesn't care.
Gabrielle is slim and lean.
Raphaelle is chubby a bit.
Gabrielle, oftentimes on a serious tone.
Raphaelle oozes her funny bones.
Gabrielle delights in strumming the ukulele.
Raphaelle sings and dances like a bumblebee.
They may differ in one way or another.
Yet they so love each other.
They love pillow fights.
They giggle to their might.
They both love to bike.
They both love to hike.
They both build blocks.
They enjoy watching vlogs.
They always cause curve lines on ones face.
They're mom's and dad's angels in disguise.

Of Love Letters and Musings

I've done my tasks for the day
I've smiled to those who come my way
And have even laughed and looked so gay
Yet, deep inside I feel so lonely
Cause it's you that I wanted to be with everyday
What keeps these times bearable
Is the thought that our love and God
Will keep us together one of these days.

****

I really love and miss your company too
And not a single day that I didn't pray I could be with
you
However, we have to live one day at a time
And abide in God who has the master plan

****

Be patient, my love
Be patient, my love
Cause we'll be together in due time
Hold on
Just hold on
And entrust everything to Thine
And we will be together soon.

****

May God be always with you as you tackle many
things each day
May He prepares refreshment and renewals for you in
the midst of activities
May He anoint your mind with His oil of tranquility
That all your activities for the day be all in harmony

****

Amidst the crowd
It is your face I see
Amidst the noise
It is your voice I heard so glee
Amidst the pouring rain
It is your warm embrace I yearn
Amidst the busy days
It is with you that I found peace

****

Thy beauty is more radiant than the stars in the vast
sky
Thy voice is sweetest of all to my ears
Thy face radiates the colors of the rainbow in me that
used to be pale

Knowing you're here to stay
Gives this heart of mine
Reasons to rejoice
I love you for you put meaning in my life
As lovely as the evening you are my love

****

My heart beats for you among the lilies in the fields.
I will spend my lifetime with you
If I would love you in the next life, I would still love you
I will spend the life God has given me with you
I prayed for love to come my way and I now have you

****

Through the years, Your love for us
You have faithfully shown
One of the greatest gift I've known
And so dear God I ask Thee
As I pray on bended knee
Bless my beloved and me
As we start to build our family

Thank You, Dear Friend

It was just a few years ago since I met you
But it seemed many years has passed and you're
always there all the way
I can't help but thank God for giving me a friend as
great as you
Being with you oftentimes is what I always pray

When I have fears and worries that I tend to hand
over
You're always there to give me encouragement and
comfort
How I wished both of us with God, could always be
together
So that I'll be brave enough to face problems of all
sort

When I've come to you to share my little triumphs and
successes
You've seemed to feel a joy to match my own
I then realized that I am so blessed
Our friendship is one of God's precious gifts I've
known

Afflictio

Sometimes

Sometimes I no longer know what I will do with my life
Sometimes I tend to lose sight of what lies beyond
Sometimes I want to get through even for just a day
Sometimes I get so inspired when I thought
everything is going well
Sometimes I just want to sit in one corner and in
solitude dwell
Sometimes I feel encumbered with boredom of my
routine
Sometimes I want to give up to the pressures I'm in
Sometimes I feel alone in a crowd
Sometimes I feel I want to go to a solitary ground
Sometimes I forgot that God who cares
No matter what I do and what I feel

Even the Thought of You

I have given my love to you for quite some time
And now that I have you, you just don't mind
What shall I do to let this feeling go?
How can I ever forget you, what shall I do?

I cherished the moment every time I see you smile
My heart has leaped for miles
What shall I do to stop thinking of you?
When I'm haunted even the thought of you

Forgive Me if I Whine

Forgive me if I whine,
and seem oblivious of my crime
Forgive me if I think unkind
At times when I'm maligned
Come to my rescue
Every time I feel so blue
Be my mighty shield
Every time I feel so defeated
Show me Your light
every time I groped for the right
Grant me patience and hope
every time I'm at the end of my rope

In the Silence of the Night

On a dark and stormy night
In the silence of my heart
An avalanche of thoughts
Run wild in my mind.
So much work pressures.
Ever-dwindling treasures.
Kilometric list of to-dos.
All these life's woes and blues.
I stop.
I look up.
I listen.
To my angels, my dearest duo,
Dear Ivan and Raphaelle.
They move me to tears.
And erase my fears.

"Be still.
The torment of the night.
Shall not encumber you.
If you believe……
If you remain in ME."

Then and there
I found peace and might.
Even on a dark and stormy night.

Reaching Out to You

Reaching out to you is all I can do
This has been my cry since I met you
I'm pretty sure this dream can hardly come true
So, I guess it's high time for me not to pursue.

I must put an end to this before I go too far
Though at times it makes me feel good but inevitably
hurts so bad
It fills up my heart then tears it apart
And it's been quite torturing even from the start.

Dimitir

When my days become so serious
Hear my heart becoming tedious
Even the beatings are furious
Never will this be harmonious.

Let heaven take its guiding light
O'er this weary and lonesome flight
Veil of scarlet cover my sight
Extreme love oh where is thy might.

As I make my leave, never cry
Never will this hand dry your eye
Do not worry and do not sigh
Heart now bids its final goodbye.

Affliction has caused me dire pain
Tension, why dost thou keep thy stain?
Emptiness has made me insane
Rivulets of sorrow pouring in the rain

Afterall

I've never expected that I would be afflicted
It seemed the whole world's tumbling down on me
Day and night, all I could do is grieve and cry.
If I were to choose between life and death, I'd pick the latter

But as I carefully looked up at your cross
I couldn't imagine the pain that we sinners have caused
I know it wasn't the nails that held you up there
Rather, it's your love for us weighed beyond compare

You ought not to suffer like that
For you are the only Son of God
Yet your love for us forever prevails
A sacrificial death that doesn't fail

Alas, I wonder how I can follow you
Without carrying up my own cross, too
How can I hear your whisper without being pierced?
Just as I must be stained by your blood if I wanted your embrace

And so, I offer you my sorrows and pains
All the adversities this life may bring
I offer you my heart and soul
For you're the master of my life, after all.

And So, I Waited

Days and months had already gone by
Yet I still have this one constant cry
I need peace, yes, an everlasting peace
In this world of tribulations and uncertainties.

How long will I wait; will it be forever?
I strive to be patient, but my human nature at
times prevail
Thanks be to God; He gives me the grace to
sustain
And I hope His promise of peace may be just
around the bend.

I wanted to give up but just couldn't allow it
How could I ever stay away from the ones I love?
We pull an act, as if grieving isn't enough
To conceal this sadness behind a mask of
happiness

I am tired and weary of life's hardships
Perhaps I have gone beyond my threshold of pain
I want to escape from this state of being
And flee from this torture I'm amassing

Afterall, I realized that God is a God of infinite goodness
He never forsakes me especially when I am in distress
He comes to the rescue and lifts my dampened soul
He is just there and all I have to do is call.

No matter what happens, I just keep on holding on
Believing in Christ's promises alone
So, now Lord I have nothing more to ask
All I want to do is to thank you for loving me that much.

Silhouette

Sun's refulgent rays I barely can see
In spite of the brightness that lights this world.
Love's potion withheld this heart to be free
Peaks and summits beckon these knees to fold.

Overflowing longing made me weary
Upon thinking of your amorous face
Eyes gushed the tears whose rhythm is dreary
Thinking if arms of mine still could embrace.

Retreating to my old path is impossible
Ever will I wander, lost and despair
Amidst the vast sea that brews in trouble
Not even a hand of yours dare to care.

Now that you are just a mere silhouette
'Ere will I, with my restless heart, regret.

Contritum Est Cor Meum In Dolore

Where do broken hearts go
When it is filled with sorrow?
Where will it find solace
When it needs a tender embrace?

Where will it find comfort and consolation
When it is left in desperate isolation?
Where will it search for its life
When it is burdened with strife?

Contritum est cor meum in dolore
Will end when it finds its Amore.
Life's sorrows come to an end
When Heart holds on Faith like a dear friend.

It banishes the darkness within
When Heart starts to love again.

All Will Be Well

Are you burdened with responsibilities?
Laden with frailties after frailties?
Do you need to endure the risks of your profession?
And perform multifaceted functions?

All will be well
All will be well!
Inner peace!
Inner peace!

Thought you've slept in the silence of the night
But your night has just begun
And yet you maintain that rare grace
And yet you keep that inner peace

That is grace beyond pressure
Grace beyond measure

Musings: Faith and Love in Times of Affliction

Bless the Lord my soul
For His anger endures not
His mercy is great
When He bore the rugged cross
He thought of you and the world

****

Man is so precious
More valuable than pure gold
The heavens rejoice
Echoing triumphant songs
Over those repentant souls

****

Man should not worry
But should live like the lilies
For the Lord keeps him
With His great love and mercy
He gives His endless blessings

****

Man should not forget
He was created by God
In His own image
With His purest affection
Made him high o'er creation

****

Man is never up
Nor is he even under
For he is equal
With the woman from his side
Both are created by God

****

How I wished
All these miseries
Was just a dream.
But in the end.
It is His ways
And not man's ways
But I always believe
All things worked together
For the good of those who loved Him
Keeping the faith here, Oh Lord.
Trying to attain even a speck of that of Job's
That no matter how tempest is the storm
He kept anchoring to the power of the Cross

****

Two yellow flowers peeking on my window
As if telling me, "Don't feel so blue
Look at the skies, they're bluer than blue"
Few birds are chirping incessantly
As if telling me, "look at us, we never go hungry
Even if we do not toil nor sow"
The sun is beaming with so much pride
As if telling me, "soon, you can have fun outside
And enjoy the summer fun like a child"

For the God Almighty sees it all
And just want His children to see
A new light
A new sight
And soon there will be healing
All over the land.

****

The clouds
Could no longer hold
Heaven's tears
It just keeps
On pouring
Until it ran out
Of tears to shed.
And wishing
The sun
Will come out
Tomorrow
And dry
The flood of tears
On Earth.
And there will be
Healing all over the land.

It's a Long Day

Yesterday was quite a LONG day

It started at four
>LONG-ing to curl up in bed
>I ended up waking at thirty minutes past four
>but it gave me time to hug and pray over
>my loved ones who are still asleep

Waited for LONG hours just to secure a government document
>but it gave me time to draft a PTA letter request
>and a birthday note for a cousin dear

Confronted with a work in progress which has been LONG overdue
>but it gave me time to file my "pile" in the office
>for it seemed I misplaced one of the docs

Got indigested with a LONG list of activities
>of my kiddos in the coming months
>but I'm grateful its objectives will redound to benefit of my kids' development

Took a very LONG route from the meeting to the terminal
>Since the driver fetched passengers of opposite directions
>but it gave me a glimpse of the city at night

Got an ankle sprain at the terminal
>despite wearing a not so LONG heeled shoes and nobody cared to help me
>but it gave me courage to stand despite the pain and shame

The Bottomline is:
      God is just testing how LONG can I stretch
      My Patience and Perseverance
      So, at the end of the day
      Am still grateful to my Creator
      Taking account of the time of my long day.

Whew! Got a LOOOOONG way to go!

Poetry Challenges Entries

Sail on the seven silver seas I dare
In search for true love I can call my own.
Hoping to find someone to hold and care
Braving gigantic waves by the wind blown.

It seems fate is lost in the horizon
In the passing of the sun, stars and moon.
Will destiny set heart free from prison?
Oh, dear heavens! Let it be very soon.

My faith is slowly dwindling and dying.
Hope is fading and becoming colder.
To hold back tears from falling I am trying.
Give me thy sweet love to make me bolder.

Love's symphony with you will be sweeter,
As we both walk the aisle of the minster.

Hay(na)ku 1

Dove
Signifies love
From heaven above

Monogamous loving bird
Never heard
Flirted

Hay(na)ku 2

Crickets
Among thickets
Noisy like markets

Evening till dawn
Praying alone
Monotone

#hayins 1

Bees
Sting tingles
Honey produced medicates

Busiest in summer
Amassing pollens
Flower-hopping

#hayins 2

Cicadas
Sing ecstatically
Loud high-pitched buzzes.

Chorus of cicadas
Breaking silence
Symphony

Modified Sonnet

Ivan D. Villaluz

Rhyme scheme: abab-cdcd-efef-gg
Meter: hexameter

Do not go calm or placid amidst this COVID
For it is permitted time to cause afflictions,
Causing all people defenseless and invalid,
Marking daily death toll trend to surge in millions.
Viewed as pandemic causing races to panic,
This strange virus has shaken mankind's existence;
Plunging down global economy so drastic.
It tested man's acclaimed knowledge and competence.
The World is busy searching for a solution.
Brilliant scientists are exerting all efforts;
Braving their battle, hoping for a remission,
Unmindful of body and mental discomforts.
If man's willing to surrender his Corona,
Merciful God will grant the whole world nirvana.

Pen and Paper Love Story

Ivan D. Villaluz

Pen and Paper had a spectacular yet fascinating fight.
Fight started when both arrogantly claimed to be more
important to people.
People are too dependent to Pen and Paper.
Paper exclaimed, "I am created far greater than a paper!"
Paper rebutted, " I am even mightier than a double-edged
sword even to this day!"
Day came by when they have to prove.
"Prove me wrong, now that you see the students reading
books."
"Books? You're right, but just take a look what is on their
hands. Isn't it a pen?"
Pen said, "Let's move on and find some more proofs.
Proofs will be out there to tell."
"Tell me, Pen if you are far better than me in hospitals."
"Hospitals have doctors that give prescriptions."
"Prescriptions are important to patients."
"Patients receive both of us in their hands as they leave."
"Leave it quits for now and let's call it a day."
Day was tiresome and long for Pen and Paper.
Paper said, "Let's take a rest under the tree."
Tree whispered, "Don't disturb the man."
Man was writing a poem dedicated to his love with a pen.
Pen said, "His poem, because of a pen is made beautiful."
"Beautiful indeed," said the tree.

Tree consoled the paper.

"Paper, don't be dismayed. The man was writing on you, too."

Too confused, they both asked the tree to decide.

"Decide? Can't you yet figure out the glow on the face of the man?"

Man exclaimed, "Thank you, Lord for these paper and pen!"

Pen and Paper looked at each other lovingly.

Lovingly a poem is written with paper and a pen.

Corona

Ivan D. Villaluz

Virulent vicious virus shaking the World
Instantaneously inflicting infirmities haunting mankind
Perplexing peoples' peace leading them to panic
Exposing egoistic enmities lurking in every heart
Raising radical racism closing boundaries, borders and
bridges.
Frequent frolic festivities coming to silence
Raging raucous rallies shouting in the streets
Overtaking our oblivious aching hearts
Making mornings' mourning echoing through the night.
Heaven's helping hand reaching every soul
Every ebullient Easter offering perfect and pure
Lamb's life-giving love bringing hope
Life's lessons learned teaching anew.
God's gracious guidance burning inside
Offering ourselves opportunities lifting our spirits
Doing daily duties lighting others' lives
Showing selfless sympathy cheering those in sorrow
Seek sacred sustenance coming from above
Purchase perfect peace gushing forth from the Prince of
Peace
Learn Lamb's loving obedience to His will
Evade envious Enemy praying for God's mercy.
Newness never numbs beating heart for others
Don't deliver disgrace hurting your brethren
Offer oneself onto caring those in need
Remember reaping righteousness giving your head a
golden crown.

#lovegravity

A winning piece

Entry 1

Love in its truest essence is Divine.
It brings sunshine and sweetest smiles.
Love I have I give to thine.
This will usher us to journey endless miles.

Love is heaven sent for the two destined soulmates.
Behold the affection of a beautiful dove.
Here have I treasured since we were schoolmates,
Willing to blame gravity to fall in love.

Entry 2

Pattering raindrops fall to drench the thirsty flora.
Withered leaves fall to nourish the soil for plants to feed
the fauna.
Tears run down the cheeks to change the face's aura.
Sweat drips down the body in the steamy sauna.

Humble prayers rise up to the highest heaven,
Pouring down God's blessings from above.
Heart beats the purest love for a maiden.
Willing to blame gravity to fall in love.

#gameonsunday

A winning piece

Waking up to the smell of the morning dew
Before it wanes when kissed by the sun's rays
Lured by the smiling flowers in variant hues
Perfect for leis or simply stack on empty vase

And before the sun yearns for a good night's rest
Candlelight dinner for two is perfectly set
Celebrating love under the moonlight
Ah, the list never ends, jewels and inspirations of a poet

#chrysalism (spelled out in pnemonics - first letters of every line)

To Live is to Love

A winning piece

Cherish moments in the womb;
Human beings take nine tranquil months inside.
Reminisce tender love and care;
Your existence is greatly valued.
Sore high with outstretched wings once you are freed;
Attune yourself with the world.
Liberate your soul from solitude;
Increase your boundless horizon.
Serve others with delight;
Make the most of your endowed gifts.
Imagine your world without love;
Solitude and sullenness will be your only friend.
Live to love with all your might
In reaching out with your heart and hand.
For you are created for this purpose
Envelope the World with your healing love.

#oddquain

A winning piece

Life,
White as snow
Marred with greed and lies
Hindering progress and peace
Death

#moodymonday

A winning piece

Gumamela
Lures butterflies
Pink in summer
Love this awesome sight
Beauty

Pink
Plumeria radiates
Reminds of summer
Enkindles love from heart
Memories

#ticklingtuesday

Ukiah 1
A winning piece

Yellow Sun greets everyone
Brings joy and laugher
Blessing all God's creation

Ukiah 2

Friendship brings good memories
Gladness to the heart
It makes life's journey lighter

UKIAH 1

Beaming rays of the sunlit
Caressed one cold cheeks
Downtrodden soul awakens

UKIAH 2

The storm is at its tempest
Chaos and panic
Need to anchor on the cross

#willpowerwednesday

Lune 1

Life's battle
Stranger like orange
Take courage

Lune 2

Bold orange
Dominant color
Marks courage

#fieryfriday

Shadorma 1

Red is Love
And so is Anger.
Things go wrong;
Things go right.
Colors can mean different things.
It's for you to choose.

Shadorma 2

Do not sleep
Over your anger.
Let it go;
Free yourself.
Paint the town with red instead.
Use your heart and head.

#agastopia

Pottery Divine

Out of the lowly earth man was created.
He was laid on the ground naked and lifeless.
Divine hands lovingly and skillfully crafted;
Perfectly designed on His image and likeness.

Having received the spirit he opened his eyes;
Stretched his
muscular arms and perfect physique.
He surveyed all the creatures and then realize;
Discovered that somehow he was definitely unique.

He was made to a slumber.
Lo and behold what he saw,
A beautiful and tender body he felt like an ember!
Exclaimed his grateful heart,
"This agastopia I have for your breasts makes me feel
unfathomable awe."

#thursdaytwist
(a winning piece)

Girls are such wonderful creatures,
they can cause men's words to twist
but leave tongues free from fractures.

Winning Piece

#chrysalism

(spelled out in pnemonics - first letters of every line)

To Live is to Love

Cherish moments in the womb;
Human beings take nine tranquil
months inside.
Reminisce tender love and care;
Your existence is greatly valued.
Sore high with outstretched wings
once you are freed;
Attune yourself with the world.
Liberate your soul from solitude;
Increase your boundless horizon.
Serve others with delight;
Make the most of your endowed gifts.
Imagine your world without love;

Solitude and sullenness will be your
only friend.
Live to love with all your might
In reaching out with your heart and hand.
For you are created for this purpose
Envelope the World with your healing love.

Jury's Review:

Ivan Villaluz poem moves very sensitively from
solitude in the womb of the mother to the life of love.
His analogy of loneliness in the womb to a life without
love is beautifully expressed. The creativity is
blooming in each sentence of this beautiful acrostic
poem.

#konectezinemonthlycontest

God's Greatest Gift
A precious heavenly gem
That I proudly wear like a golden diadem
Is my beautiful and loving Mother,
A woman like no other.
She lovingly cuddles me
And always makes me glee.
Her lullabies keep me still
And cares for me when I get ill.
Her sticks truly made me weep
But good fruits now I reap.
She cries with me over my failures,

And reminds me that someday they will be my treasures.
She tells me to rise every time I fall,
Encourages me to stand tall.
She reminds me that life is a journey
And that obstacles along the way are many.
will cherish her nuggets of wisdom
For these will give me the freedom.
Among God's greatest gifts is my mother,
A woman like no other.

#magicmonday

I am under the influence of your love's spell.
I just hope my life will still be well.
Your sweetest smiles drowned me to deepest trench of the ocean.
This heart has drunk your love's magical potion.
I do not want to escape your tender embrace.
I just want to be lost in your world without a trace.
Your gentle voice whispering my ears.
Banish all my worries and fears.
Wake me not in this wonderful dream
Even if the moon loses its beam.
Oh, my Love let our hearts sing in symphony
And let our hearts beat in orchestrated harmony.

#acrosticlove

FONDNESS (Acrostics combined with chain)
For true love's kiss is longingly remembered often
Often reminds feelings that are nostalgic
Nostalgic to the heart and mind so it will never experience death
Death has no power over it for true love ends never
Never can time and space erase
Erase the memories and you will regret soon
Soon you will realize that love is even felt sweeter
Sweeter because it was why it was created for.

#wittyclerihew

I am Judas Escariot
For thirty pieces of silver and dire greed I became an idiot.
And why do you think I hanged myself on a tree?
Cursed was my birth and destiny; thus, I can't set myself free.

I am Peter.
Thrice have I denied the Lord then crowed the rooster.
With my dwindling faith I almost got drowned,
Afraid of the turbulent waves that surround.

#lovemakeslifelive

In the beginning there was Love
And Love begets Life
And Life started to live
But Life is faced with all sorts of trials
Yet Love hopes and believes, thus he never fails Life
Life has to face challenges and must continue the
race
And there was Love ready to embrace
Life's journey was dreary and long
But Love endures and was patient all along
Life's ups and downs are despising and crippling
But Love keeps him smiling
There were many times that Life wants to surrender
But Love kept pushing Life up from down under
Love was there through thick and thin
So, Life found the strength within
Love makes Life live

And Life makes Love alive.

#altermatter

As I stare at the window, I see myself enter
Blowing gently on the lazy curtain.
I'll be around until the twelfth of never.
This I can be certain.
I run freely here and there
Touching the leaves as I pass by.
I love to spread the flowers' scent everywhere
For all the passers-by.

I give the fluffy clouds their different shapes.
Sometimes creating fancy figures for children at play.
You feel me swaying with the flowers in the
landscapes.
Yes, I enjoy it, but I seldom stay. You feel me in the
cold breeze of early dawn.
I charge the seas and they wave back at me.
Children want their kites to be blown.
And I serve them to set their spirits free.
Sometimes I quiet myself and retire.
Sometimes I unleash my anger.
When tired I do not have the desire.
When angry I put everything in my path in danger.
Well, this you should know: That is truly me!
It depends on how you deal and show—
A friend or a foe to you I can be.

#novelpoem

Tribute to Mothers (On Mother's Day)

Amiable Eyes Illuminate her Overwhelming and
Unparalleled beauty
Envelop her Innermost Observable and Undeniably
desirable Attitude
Inspiring Others to Understand and Appreciate
Everyone's value and dignity
Oasis of love and Unfailing Affection Emanating
Innately among all mothers
Unquestionably Accepting her children's Errors and
Instilling discipline and Obedience.

#fridayflavour

Cheeks as luscious as strawberries,
Lips as red as cherries,
Scent as fragrant as vanilla,
Eyes as sparkling as crystal ice,
Oh, so rich and flavorful, a lady with her enchanting
smile.

#mysticalmonday

TRIALS lead to TRAILS of success.
HATREDS are HARDEST THREADS to cut.
When life at NIGHT is CHEATING, one THING is for sure.
It's TEACHING the BUILDER to REBUILD.
One OUGHT to LIVE life even when it gets TOUGH,
for EVIL days will come to END in a lion's DEN.

#saturdaysplash

Dreams usher long lost memories
Splashing out happy thoughts of you
Enkindles the fire and desire
Lurking in the chambers of my lonely heart.

Consummatum est

In the beginning there was love
For God's perfect love begets love.
God's immeasurable love created
The universe and all its array
With splendor and glory interplay.
The first fall in the Garden of Eden
Brought curse to all men and women
To suffer and endure affliction and pain.
Thus, cursed be our destiny ordained.
Treading the journey,
As couples may be hard as it seems,
Yet Love will see God's guiding light as it beams.
Faith will be the guiding star every step of the way
And Hope will keep stirring night and day.
"Consummatum est"
On the triumphant cross was uttered
Giving us assurance
That by His great love He conquered.
Trials, tribulations and afflictions
Can neither vanish nor destroy
Heart's pure and sincere affections.
Love endures and never ends
For it is the greatest among the three Friends.
So, when you think it is time to end,
Think of Him you will greatly offend.
So, keep the faith until the end.

About the Authors

While Rosario deals with figures and spreadsheets, Ivan endures the noise and laughter of his pupils, in the exigency of their sworn duty for the State. In between, the couple dabble in poetry and free verses.

One day, a Fairy Bard dropped at their doorstep Elated, Rosario presented her poetry and verses and the rest was history.

She managed to guest write on the book,
Bards from the Far East: Anthology of Haiku and Kindred Verses from her collection of poems carefully knitted over the years.

These two souls revel in weaving poetry at its best, wrapped it up into a book of poems and verses which finally gave birth to *Semper Fi*.

About the Artist

Ssareeta Singh of India writes under the name Sherry. She is an educator, author of an upcoming book and two anthologies, and a life influencer. Her passion includes doing artwork, loving animals, and championing social causes through NGOs. She is deeply involved in creating positive impact on the lives of women and children through her trainings.

Ssareeta is also a certified super brain trainer by the world's #1 brain coach, Jim Kwik. She is a mother of three awesome sons who always keep her inspired.

About the Editor

Ayo Gutierrez pens her art in the Philippines. Her poems have been published in more than 15 books that are sold on Amazon and other online platforms. She is the author of Yearnings & Evocare, among others, and co-author of the Amazon bestseller, *Almost is the Same as Never Second Edition.*

Ayo owns GMGA Entertainment Productions and GMGA Publishing. For more information, you may visit her Facebook Page: GMGA Publishing.

We appreciate receiving your review of our book on Amazon.

Semper fi,
Ivan and Rosario

Notes

Notes